GOD

SPEAKS THROUGH

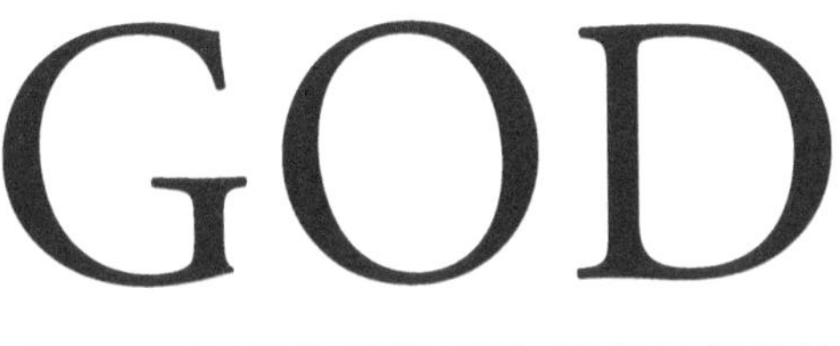

Quotes

Tony Eason

ISBN 979-8-89043-037-3 (paperback)
ISBN 979-8-89043-038-0 (digital)

Christian Faith Publishing
832 Park Avenue
Meadville, PA 16335
www.christianfaithpublishing.com

Printed in the United States of America

Satan cannot make you sin;
sin is a choice. (Tony Eason)

2

Chasing things in this world
will only lead to despair and
disappointment. (Tony Eason)

3

Pray and make the devil
tremble. (Tony Eason)

You don't have to pray smart
or educated prayers to God
because he understands
all prayers whether smart,
educated, or uneducated.
(Tony Eason)

You're not in competition
with others when you pray.
Just pray, and let the Holy
Spirit lead you. (Tony Eason)

God can rehab your life;
he is your rehabilitation
source. (Tony Eason)

7

Satan isn't after your accomplishments, your money, your job, your fancy cars, or your big house; he is after your soul. (Tony Eason)

Limit your friendship circle,
and you will lessen the
drama! (Tony Eason)

Having one loyal friend is
superior to having a thousand
disloyal ones. (Tony Eason)

In a world with so much
brokenness, friendships matter.
Friends help mold us into the
exact person God intended
us to be. (Tony Eason)

11

The purest kind of love is
godly love. (Tony Eason)

12

Where does my hope come
from? I can only point to
the cross. (Tony Eason)

13

If you want to do something positive with social media, make it more about *Jesus* and less about you. (Tony Eason)

Christians are on *display*, and the world is watching how you act, what you say, and what you do. (Tony Eason)

15

No church is perfect, and if
you are looking for a perfect
church, then you are looking for
perfect people, and sad to say
there is neither. (Tony Eason)

16

God is neither Republican nor Democrat; his *throne* is above both. (Tony Eason)

I trust God totally, but I don't
always trust myself to do the
right thing. Self is the problem,
not God. (Tony Eason)

18

Church can't save you,
but it can route you in the
right direction toward *Jesus*
who can! (Tony Eason)

19

The Ten Commandments
are linked together like
a chain; if you break one
commandment, you've broken
them all. (Tony Eason)

# 20

Love is God's love
language. (Tony Eason)

If you want to be transformed
into the person that God wants
you to be, the Bible is a good
place to start. (Tony Eason)

22

Christianity is not a label; it's not a name tag that you can just pin on and go on your way. Christianity has meaning, and Jesus Christ paid a "big price" for it by dying on the cross for our sins. (Tony Eason)

To be a follower of Jesus; he's
got to be the One doing the
leading, not you. (Tony Eason)

24

If going to church seems like a chore, then you're going for the wrong reason. (Tony Eason)

25

How you live your life
now will determine your
eternal home, your eternal
destiny. (Tony Eason)

There will come a time
when you must distance
yourself from rude and toxic
people, but always pray
for them. (Tony Eason)

Without God as our
foundation, life is
meaningless. (Tony Eason)

28

Focusing on worldly possessions will never satisfy you; only God can fill that void. (Tony Eason)

If God can't change your life,
then Satan will. (Tony Eason)

30

Don't ever put a pastor on a
pedestal and don't ever put
a pastor above God's throne
because some people tend
to follow the pastor and
not God. (Tony Eason)

31

When God is in your head,
Satan has no room to plant
seeds. (Tony Eason)

32

When you go all in with God,
you will never be looked at
the same by those who don't
know him. (Tony Eason)

33

When family and friends
abandon you, run to
Jesus. (Tony Eason)

Some Christians have no
problem loving people in their
inner circle; it's the people
in their outer circle who are
overlooked. They are the ones in
this world who are broken and
are in desperate need of prayer,
love, and hope. (Tony Eason)

35

To get to heaven, you
got to go through Jesus
first. (Tony Eason)

If the world hates you because
you're a Christ follower, then
you're in good company because
it hated *Jesus* first. (Tony Eason)

37

Here's a trustworthy saying:
God created me. He sent
his son, Jesus, to die for me,
and He raised him from
the dead. (Tony Eason)

When God is at the center
of your life, he changes
everything. (Tony Eason)

39

All police officers are not
evil, but there are evil police
officers; every black person isn't
evil, but there are evil black
people. Every white person isn't
evil, but there are evil white
people; every person of color
isn't evil, but there are evil
people of color. (Tony Eason)

40

The devil snoops around
until he finds your
weakest temptation, and
then he launches his
attacks. (Tony Eason)

Don't play God in church
and act like the world out
there! (Tony Eason)

There are two doors to choose from before you die: a door to "heaven" and a door to "hell." Choose wisely because your choice will depend on where you will spend eternity. (Tony Eason)

43

If you hang with God long
enough, he will transform
your life. (Tony Eason)

Social media is a great way to
minister to a lost world that
has millions of people, so do
your part and let God finish
the impossible. Let Him finish
what you started! (Tony Eason)

45

While writing the story
of your life, let God hold
the pen. (Tony Eason)

When life knocks you down,
get back up again and again
until you're standing strong
again. (Tony Eason)

The Bible is a road map to
a world that needs to be
transformed. (Tony Eason)

God is the world's GPS; He is
tracking you daily. (Tony Eason)

49

Jesus went after the one and not the ninety-nine. You are that one. (Tony Eason)

Jesus serves as the remedy
for the afflictions that the
world is desperately suffering
from. (Tony Eason)

If Jesus thought that it was
necessary to pray to the Father
in heaven, then we humans
ought to indeed pray. Prayer
is powerful! (Tony Eason)

Satan is ever present, trying
to destroy our glory and
remove our crown. One of
his most powerful tools is
discouragement. Don't let your
discouragement make Satan
rejoice. (Marvin J. Ashton)

If you're helping someone
and expecting something in
return, you're doing business,
not kindness. (Unknown)

3

You may not know what you are
going to do; you only know that
God knows what He is going
to do. (Oswald Chambers)

Never let loneliness drive
you back to toxic people.
(Third Eye Thoughts)

Our purpose in life is to know God and make God known. (Randall Darby)

To walk out of God's will is to step into nowhere. (C. S Lewis)

God deserves first place in
your life, and you deserve the
experience of putting Him
there. (Criswell Freeman)

8

When you enroll in the "school of faith," you never know what may happen next. The life of faith presents challenges that keep you going and keep you growing! (Warren Wiersbe)

# 9

Joy is the serious business
of heaven. (C.S Lewis)

10

God help the man that
won't marry until he finds
a perfect woman, and God
help him still more if he finds
her. (Benjamin Tillett)

11

If you expect perfection from
people, your whole life is a
series of disappointments,
grumblings, and complaints.
(Bruce Barton)

There is no greater lie than
a truth misunderstood.
(William James)

13

A Christian is never in a
state of completion but
always in the process of
becoming. (Martin Luther)

14

The devil is a better theologian
than any of us and is a
devil still. (A. W. Tozer)

15

Christianity is neither
Democratic nor Republican—
it's better than both.
(Stephen Mattson)

What is the use of being
famous on earth? when
heaven doesn't know your
name. (Billy Graham)

17

Go to church once a week and nobody pays attention. Worship God 7 days a week and you become strange! (A. W. Tozer)

18

God is looking for people to use, and if you can get usable, he will wear you out. The most dangerous prayer you can pray is this: "Use me". (Rick Warren)

# 19

Some people will never like you because your spirit irritates their demons. (Denzel Washington)

20

He who passively accepts
evil is as much involved in it
as he who helps perpetuate
it. He who accepts evil
without protesting it is
really cooperating with it.
(Martin Luther King Jr.)

21

If you can't fly then run, if
you can't run then walk, if
you can't walk then crawl,
but whatever you do you
have to keep moving forward.
(Martin Luther King Jr.)

22

Be careful what you ask for
because when you pray for rain,
you got to deal with the mud
as well. (Denzel Washington)

23

Most people pray to be blessed. Few pray to be broken. (Leonard Ravenhill)

24

The greatest answer to
prayer is more prayer.
(Samuel Chadwick)

When possessions become our
god, we become materialistic
and greedy…and we forfeit
our contentment and our
joy. (Charles Swindoll)

If you only pray when
you're in trouble…you're
in trouble. (Unknown)

27

We cannot pray in love and live
in hate and still think we are
worshiping God. (A. W. Tozer)

28

Jesus is not one of many ways
to approach God, nor is He the
best way of several ways. He
is the only way. (A.W. Tozer)

29

God would rather have a
man on the wrong side of the
fence than on the fence. The
worst enemies of the apostles
are not the opposers but the
appeasers. (Vance Havner)

30

God never promised to
remove us from our struggles.
He does promise, however,
to change the way we look
at them. (Max Lucado)

People are watching the way we act, more than they are listening to what we say. (Max Lucado)

No one can pray and worry at
the same time. (Max Lucado)

33

A person with no devotional
life generally struggles
with faith and obedience.
(Charles Stanley)

34

Prayer may not get us what we want, but it will teach us to want what we need. (Vance Havner)

35

You can't light another's path
without casting light on
your own. (John Maxwell)

36

God will never reject you.
Whether you accept Him is
your decision. (Charles Stanley)

37

Prayer is the most important
tool for your mission to this
world. People may refuse our
love or reject our message, but
they are defenseless against
our prayers. (Rick Warren)

38

By not forgiving, by not letting wrongs go, we aren't getting back at anyone. We are merely barricading our own hearts. (Jim Cymbala)

39

In God's plan, God is the standard for perfection. We don't compare ourselves to others; they are just as fouled up as we are. The goal is to be like Him; anything less is inadequate. (Max Lucado)

40

The Bible is offensive to those who are offended by its message. (Manny Pacquiao)

You have to say yes to God first
before you can effectively say no
to the devil. (Vance Havner)

The devil keeps so many of us
stuck in our weaknesses. He
reminds us of our pasts when
we ought to remind him of
his future—he doesn't have
one. (Franklin Graham)

43

Don't worry about what you
do not understand. Worry
about what you do understand
in the Bible but do not live
by. (Corrie ten Boom)

You must never sacrifice
your relationship with
God for the sake of a
relationship with another
person. (Charles Stanley)

45

A man who is intimate with
God is not intimidated by
man. (Leonard Ravenhill)

46

As we seek to become disciples
of Jesus Christ, we should
never forget that the word
disciple is directly related
to the word discipline. To
be a disciple of the Lord
Jesus Christ is to know His
discipline. (Dennis Swanberg)

Our lives are full of potholes,
and we have a choice to either
go around them or tackle
them head on. (Tony Eason)

You have some people that
will encourage you, and you
have some that will sit on the
sidelines and watch and hope
that you fail. (Tony Eason)

3

If you are struggling with the difficulties of life, do a self-audit of you to find out why, the answer could be buried deep within. (Tony Eason)

4

When your biggest
encourager is you, be okay
with that! (Tony Eason)

5

It takes a certain discipline to keep the same mindset day in and day out. (Tony Eason)

6

If you aren't winning, you're losing. (Tony Eason)

To be the best version of
yourself, you must train
your mind, body, and
spirit. (Tony Eason)

8

To be consistent in
what you do, you must
develop a consistent
mindset. (Tony Eason)

Bible Verses to Reflect On!

1

John 3:16 (NIV)

For God so loved the world that he gave his one and only Son, that whoever believes in him shall not perish but have eternal life.

2

Jeremiah 29:11 (NIV)

"For I know the plans I have for you," declares the Lord, "plans to prosper you and not to harm you, plans to give you hope and a future."

3

Romans 8:28 (NIV)

And we know that in all things God works for the good of those who love him, who have been called according to his purpose.

4

Psalm 23:4 (NIV)

Even though I walk through the darkest valley, I will fear no evil, for you are with me; your rod and your staff, they comfort me.

Romans 12:2 (NIV)

Do not conform to the pattern of this world, but be transformed by the renewing of your mind. Then you will be able to test and approve what God's will is—his good, pleasing and perfect will.

6

Philippians 4:6 (NIV)

Do not be anxious about anything, but in every situation, by prayer and petition, with thanksgiving, present your requests to God.

7

Ephesians 6:12 (NIV)

For our struggle is not against flesh and blood, but against the rulers, against the authorities, against the powers of this dark world and against the spiritual forces of evil in the heavenly realms.

8

Isaiah 41:10 (NIV)

So do not fear, for I am with you; do not be dismayed, for I am your God. I will strengthen you and help you; I will uphold you with my righteous right hand.

9

Philippians 4:8 (NIV)

Finally, brothers and sisters, whatever is true, whatever is noble, whatever is right, whatever is pure, whatever is lovely, whatever is admirable—if anything is excellent or praiseworthy—think about such things.

10

Joshua 1:9 (NIV)

Have I not commanded you? Be strong and courageous. Do not be afraid; do not be discouraged, for the LORD your God will be with you wherever you go.

11

John 16:33 (NIV)

I have told you these things, so that in me you may have peace. In this world you will have trouble. But take heart! I have overcome the world.

12

John 14:6 (NIV)

Jesus answered, "I am the way and the truth and the life. No one comes to the Father except through me."

13

Isaiah 40:31 (NIV)

But those who hope in the LORD will renew their strength. They will soar on wings like eagles; they will run and not grow weary, they will walk and not be faint.

14

1 Peter 5:7 (NIV)

Cast all your anxiety on him because he cares for you.

15

Matthew 11:28 (NIV)

Come to me, all you who are weary and burdened, and I will give you rest.

16

Psalm 91:1 (NIV)

Whoever dwells in the shelter of the Most High will rest in the shadow of the Almighty.

17

Genesis 1:27 (NIV)

So God created mankind in his own image, in the image of God he created them; male and female he created them.

18

1 Corinthians 13:4 (NIV)

Love is patient, love is kind. It does not envy, it does not boast, it is not proud.

19

1 Thessalonians 5:18 (NIV)

Give thanks in all circumstances; for this is God's will for you in Christ Jesus.

20

Romans 5:8 (NIV)

But God demonstrates his own love for us in this: While we were still sinners, Christ died for us.

21

1 Peter 5:8 (NIV)

Be alert and of sober mind. Your enemy the devil prowls around like a roaring lion looking for someone to devour.

22

Ephesians 6:18 (NIV)

And pray in the Spirit on all occasions with all kinds of prayers and requests. With this in mind, be alert and always keep on praying for all the Lord's people.

23

Romans 8:39 (NIV)

Neither height nor depth, nor anything else in all creation, will be able to separate us from the love of God that is in Christ Jesus our Lord.

24

Ephesians 4:32 (NIV)

Be kind and compassionate to one another, forgiving each other, just as in Christ God forgave you.

25

Galatians 5:22 (NIV)

But the fruit of the Spirit is love, joy, peace, forbearance, kindness, goodness, faithfulness.

26

Galatians 5:23 (NIV)

Gentleness and self-control. Against such things there is no law.

27

1 Timothy 1:15 (NIV)

Here is a trustworthy saying that deserves full acceptance: Christ Jesus came into the world to save sinners—of whom I am the worst.

28

Matthew 10:28 (NIV)

Do not be afraid of those who kill the body but cannot kill the soul. Rather, be afraid of the One who can destroy both soul and the body in hell.

29

2 Chronicles 7:14 (NIV)

If my people, who are called by my name, will humble them-selves and pray and seek my face and turn from their wicked ways, then I will hear from heaven, and I will forgive their sin and will heal their land.

30

Hebrews 4:12 (NIV)

For the word of God is alive and active. Sharper than any double-edged sword, it penetrates even to dividing soul and spirit, joints and marrow; it judges the thoughts and attitudes of the heart.

(Romans 1:20 NLT)

For ever since the world was created, people have seen the earth and the sky. Through everything God made, they can clearly see his invisible quali-ties-his eternal power and divine nature. So, they have no excuse for not knowing God.

About the Author

Tony Eason is a husband, a father of three adult children, a grandfather of four children, and a brother to eight siblings, him being the ninth. Tony is a Christian and was raised in a Christian home. His parents were disciplinarians. His mother was a housewife, and his dad worked on a farm. Both are now deceased. Tony grew up in a small town of about one thousand two hundred people. There wasn't much to do there after graduating high school, so a few months after, he went into the military in midsummer of that year. During his military/government tenure, he has gotten to see and visit some great countries, such as Germany, Spain, Iraq, and Korea. All are nice places to visit, but neither country trumps the great United States. He didn't care much about English in high school, so he wasn't a big fan of writing. He did enjoy playing football, running track, and basketball, but English was not his favorite subject. Yet years later, here he is, writing his second and possibly final book. Glory be to God.